uneven parallel bars

Consultant

Kathleen Shelly, Assistant Professor
Women's Physical Education
Sacramento State College
Sacramento, California

Demonstrator

Barbara Parcher
Sacramento State College

published by:
The Athletic Institute
200 Castlewood Drive
North Palm Beach, Florida 33408

*A not-for-profit organization
devoted to the advancement of
athletics, physical education
and recreation*

Robert G. Bluth, editor

**Library of Congress
Catalog Card Number 79-109498**

**"Sports Techniques" Series
87670-078-4**

Published by The Athletic Institute
200 Castlewood Drive
North Palm Beach, Florida 33408

Foreword

The SPORTS TECHNIQUES SERIES is but one item in a comprehensive list of sports instructional aids which are made available by The Athletic Institute. This book is part of a master plan which seeks to make the benefits of athletics, physical education and recreation available to everyone.

The Athletic Institute is a not-for-profit organization devoted to the advancement of athletics, physical education and recreation. The Institute believes that participation in athletics and recreation has benefits of inestimable value to the individual and to the community.

The nature and scope of the many Institute programs are determined by a *Professional Advisory Committee,* whose members are noted for their outstanding knowledge, experience and ability in the fields of athletics, physical education and recreation.

The Institute believes that through this book the reader will become a better performer, skilled in the fundamentals of this fine event. Knowledge and the practice necessary to mold knowledge into playing ability are the keys to real enjoyment in playing any game or sport.

Gymnastics aids in the development of motor skills, flexibility, agility and endurance as well as providing enjoyable recreation.

Donald E. Bushore
Executive Director
The Athletic Institute

Introduction

The uneven parallel bars are presented using beginning and intermediate skills. It would be impossible to show every move of these levels in these few pages. Each skill is presented with the intention that it will be used as a basic or lead-up skill, with good control and form so that the gymnast may progress to more advanced skills and some creative work. Most of these skills may be done on either the low or high bar; but they should be practiced on the low bar before going up to the high bar.

Uneven parallel bars provide an opportunity for beginners to become acquainted with suspension and swinging movements. Static stunts should be discouraged. As soon as a gymnast has acquired the ability to do a particular stunt, she should be encouraged to put it with another. A routine on the bars should cover both bars, have predominantly swinging movements, show grip changes, face both directions at some time and be continuous.

Kathy Shelly

Table of Contents

grips

Regular Grip

(thumbs may or may not be around bar according to the preference of the performer)

Reverse Grip

Overgrip

Undergrip

Mixed Grip

Crossed Mixed Grip

(hands will be reversed if turn
is in opposite direction)

positions

Front Support

Rear Support

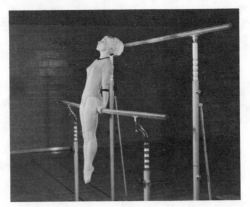

Stride Support

Front Lying Support

Rear Lying Support

Long Hang

mounts

In competition, the importance of *the mount* is to get onto the bars as cleanly and impressively as possible without using a mount of such difficulty that there is a chance of missing and falling onto or off the bars.

Long Hang to Straddle over Low Bar

Jump to grip the high bar for a long hang. Swing hips toward the low bar. With the swinging of the hips, pull back with the arms and bend at the hips with the legs straddled. Keep the hips high as they pass over the low bar.

Pull legs together and assume a rear lying position. You may choose to tuck or pike over low bar.

1. JUMP TO GRIP BAR FOR LONG HANG.
2. SWING HIPS TOWARD LOW BAR.
3. WITH HIP SWING, PULL BACK WITH ARMS AND BEND AT HIPS AS LEGS STRADDLE.
4. KEEP HIPS HIGH AS THEY PASS OVER LOW BAR.
5. PULL LEGS TOGETHER AND ASSUME A REAR LYING POSITION.

Back Hip Pullover

This mount may be performed from either side of the low bar.

With hands in a regular grip, stand facing the low bar. Elbows are bent and chest is close to the bar. Swing one leg forward and upward as you push off with the opposite leg.

Keep both knees straight for the swing. Pull with arms to position the hips near the low bar. Rotate around the low bar to come to a front support position.

1. **FACE LOW BAR WITH HANDS IN REGULAR GRIP.**
2. **ELBOWS ARE BENT AND CHEST IS CLOSE TO BAR.**
3. **SWING ONE LEG FORWARD AND UPWARD WHILE PUSHING OFF WITH OPPOSITE LEG.**
4. **KEEP KNEES STRAIGHT FOR SWING.**
5. **PULL ARMS TO POSITION HIPS NEAR LOW BAR.**
6. **ROTATE AROUND LOW BAR TO END IN FRONT SUPPORT POSITION.**

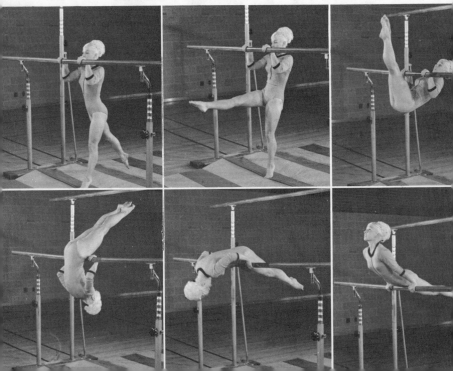

Mixed Grip Thigh Turn

From an oblique angle, stand behind the high bar. Jump to a long hang position using a mixed grip.

Swing the inside leg upward, between the bars and onto the low bar to rest the back of the thigh on the low bar. Turn toward the inside leg while lifting the outside leg to cross over the inside leg and low bar.

Release the outside hand as the body twists to regrasp the bar with a regular grip.

1. STAND AT OBLIQUE ANGLE TO HIGH BAR.
2. JUMP TO LONG HANG USING MIXED GRIP.
3. SWING INSIDE LEG UPWARD, BETWEEN BARS AND ONTO LOW BAR AT BACK OF THIGH.

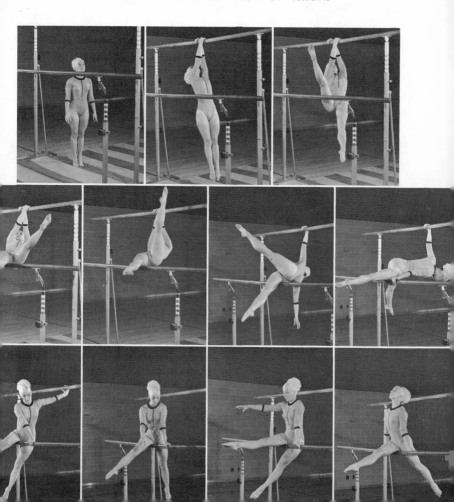

4. TURN TOWARD INSIDE WHILE LIFTING OUTSIDE LEG TO CROSS OVER INSIDE LEG AND LOW BAR.
5. RELEASE OUTSIDE HAND AS BODY TWISTS TO REGRASP BAR WITH REGULAR GRIP.

Free Front Support to Back Hip Circle

Stand facing the low bar. Jump to a free front support position on the low bar using a regular grip.

Extend both legs under the bar, lean back and follow your head backward to rotate the body around the bar on the hips.

Complete the rotation into a front support position.

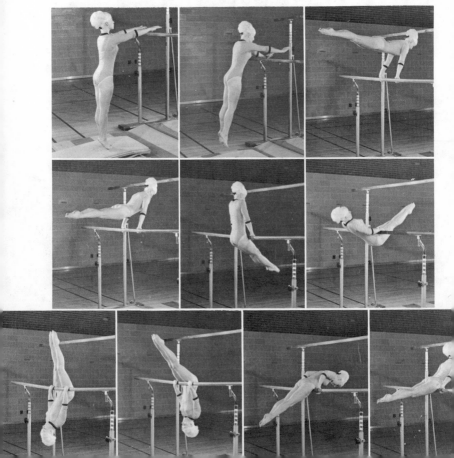

1. STAND FACING LOW BAR.
2. JUMP TO FREE FRONT SUPPORT POSITION ON LOW BAR USING REGULAR GRIP.
3. EXTEND LEGS UNDER BAR, LEAN BACK AND FOLLOW HEAD AROUND BAR WITH BODY, ROTATING ON HIPS.
4. COMPLETE ROTATION INTO FRONT SUPPORT POSITION.

Glide Kip

Stand facing the low bar. Jump to grasp the bar with a regular grip (slight overgrip). Body is in pike position with feet about two inches off the ground.

Extend the body under the bar. By bending at hips, bring toes to low bar while keeping your arms straight. Raise the upper body to the bar by pulling the bar toward the hips as legs move downward.

Finish this count in a front support position.

1. STAND FACING LOW BAR.
2. JUMP TO GRASP BAR USING REGULAR GRIP WITH SLIGHT OVERGRIP. BODY PIKES, FEET TWO INCHES OFF FLOOR.
3. EXTEND BODY UNDER BAR.
4. AT FULL EXTENSION, PROJECT FEET TOWARD LOW BAR, KEEPING ARMS STRAIGHT.

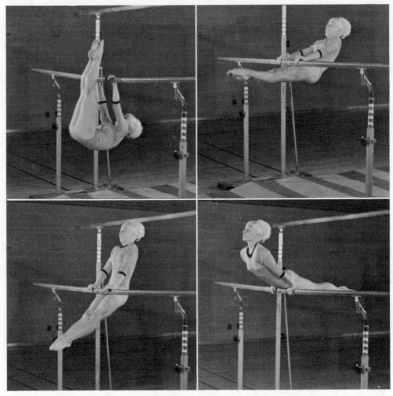

5. RAISE UPPER BODY TO BAR BY PULLING BAR TOWARD HIPS AS LEGS MOVE DOWNWARD, ARMS STAY STRAIGHT.

6. END MOUNT IN FRONT SUPPORT POSITION.

Glide, Single Leg Rise

Stand facing the low bar. Jump with pike. Again, feet are about two inches off the floor. Hands are in a regular grip with slight overgrip.

Extend the body under the bar. As the body reaches full extension, quickly bring one leg up between the arms, keeping leg close to upper body. With arms straight, pull the upper body upward, behind the bar while keeping the bar at the upper thigh portion of the back leg.

End mount in a stride position.

1. STAND FACING LOW BAR.
2. JUMP WITH PIKE. FEET ABOUT TWO INCHES OFF FLOOR. HANDS IN REGULAR GRIP WITH SLIGHT OVERGRIP.
3. EXTEND BODY UNDER BAR.
4. AS BODY REACHES FULL EXTENSION, QUICKLY BRING ONE LEG UP, BETWEEN ARMS.
5. WITH ARMS STRAIGHT, PULL UPPER BODY UPWARD BEHIND BAR WHILE KEEPING BAR AT UPPER THIGH PORTION OF BACK LEG.
6. END MOUNT IN STRIDE POSITION.

movements

The movements described are those which make up the body of the routine. They should be fluid and continuous, with no stops between movements. They should be combined so that the performer faces different directions, and works on both bars. There should be movements which change grips as well as those which change points of support (hips, feet, rear).

Kick over High Bar

From a rear lying position, support one leg upon the ball of the foot on the low bar while extending the opposite leg straight.

Kick the straight leg up and over the high bar as you push off from the low bar with the bent leg. The arms pull the hips toward the high bar as the leg kicks.

The legs come together as the body rotates backward (following the feet) around the high bar to end in a front support position on the high bar.

1. **FROM REAR LYING POSITION, SUPPORT ONE LEG UPON BALL OF FOOT ON LOW BAR WHILE EXTENDING THE OPPOSITE LEG STRAIGHT.**
2. **KICK THE STRAIGHT LEG UP AND OVER HIGH BAR WHILE PUSHING FROM LOW BAR WITH BENT LEG.**
3. **ARMS PULL TOWARD HIGH BAR AS LEG KICKS.**
4. **LEGS COME TOGETHER AS BODY ROTATES AROUND HIGH BAR BACKWARD.**
5. **FINISH IN FRONT SUPPORT POSITION ON HIGH BAR.**

Single Leg Stem Rise

From a rear lying position, extend one leg straight and bend the other leg to rest the ball of the foot on the low bar.

Swing the straight leg up toward the high bar. While keeping the arms straight, push with the bent leg to position the body behind the high bar. The straight leg swings down to meet the bent leg as you push off the low bar with that leg.

Upper body rises behind bar, leans forward and ends in front support on high bar.

1. **FROM REAR LYING POSITION, EXTEND ONE LEG STRAIGHT AND BEND OPPOSITE LEG TO REST BALL OF FOOT ON LOW BAR.**
2. **SWING STRAIGHT LEG UP TOWARD HIGH BAR.**
3. **WHILE KEEPING ARMS STRAIGHT, PUSH WITH BENT LEG TO POSITION BODY BEHIND HIGH BAR.**
4. **STRAIGHT LEG SWINGS DOWN TO MEET BENT LEG WHICH PUSHES OFF LOW BAR.**
5. **BODY SWINGS UNDER HIGH BAR TO FINISH IN FRONT SUPPORT ON HIGH BAR.**

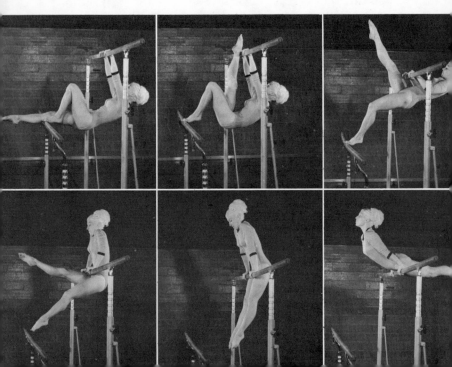

Double Leg Stem Rise

With a regular grip on the high bar, the body is in a pike position. The balls of both feet rest on the low bar.

Bend and then straighten the knees to swing the body back from the low bar while pulling hips toward the high bar with straight arms. As the body rises behind the high bar, push off the low bar with both feet.

Keep your body leaning forward over the high bar. Finish movement with a front support on the high bar.

1. WITH REGULAR GRIP ON HIGH BAR, BODY IS IN PIKE POSITION. BALLS OF FEET REST ON LOW BAR.
2. BEND AND STRAIGHTEN KNEES TO PUSH BODY BACK FROM LOW BAR WHILE PULLING HIPS TOWARD HIGH BAR WITH ARMS STRAIGHT.
3. AS BODY RISES BEHIND HIGH BAR, PUSH OFF LOW BAR WITH BOTH FEET.
4. KEEP BODY LEANING FORWARD OVER HIGH BAR.
5. FINISH MOVEMENT IN FRONT SUPPORT ON HIGH BAR.

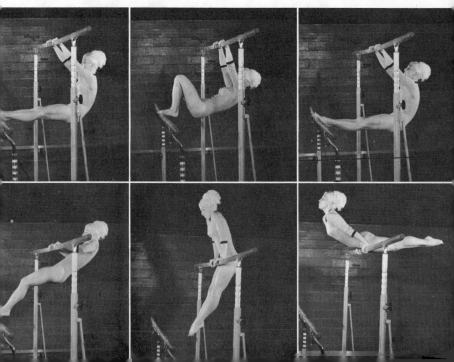

Cast (or Buck)

May be done on either bar. Grasp bar with regular grip. From a front support position, swing the legs underneath the bar and then back to lift the body off the bar with the back straight.

Keep arms straight and shoulders in front of the bar. The body should be horizontal to the floor in a free front support position.

The cast is basically a transitional movement, preparatory to other moves, therefore the concluding position may vary depending on what is to follow.

1. GRASP BAR WITH REGULAR GRIP.
2. FROM FRONT SUPPORT POSITION, SWING LEGS UNDERNEATH BAR, THEN BACK TO LIFT BODY OFF BAR WITH BACK STRAIGHT.
3. KEEP ARMS STRAIGHT AND SHOULDERS IN FRONT OF BAR.
4. THE BODY IS HORIZONTAL TO THE FLOOR IN A FREE FRONT SUPPORT POSITION.

Forward Leg Circle
(Mill or Crotch Circle)

Hands grasp low bar with reverse grip. Extend one leg between your hands and the other behind the bar in a stride position.

With head up and arms straight, lift body away from the bar. Lift the front leg and lean forward to start the rotation around the low bar while keeping your body "stretched."

The bar stays between the legs near the upper thigh or crotch, not the knee. The hands slide around the bar to return on top where the grip is tightened to stop the forward momentum.

Return to the starting position to conclude this movement.

1. GRASP LOW BAR WITH REVERSE GRIP. EXTEND ONE LEG BETWEEN HANDS AND THE OTHER BEHIND BAR IN STRIDE POSITION.
2. WITH HEAD UP AND ARMS STRAIGHT, LIFT BODY AWAY FROM BAR.
3. LIFT FRONT LEG AND LEAN FORWARD TO START ROTATION AROUND BAR. BAR STAYS BETWEEN LEGS NEAR UPPER THIGH OR CROTCH.
4. HANDS SLIDE AROUND BAR TO RETURN ON TOP WHERE GRIP IS TIGHTENED TO SLOW MOMENTUM.
5. RETURN TO STARTING POSITION.

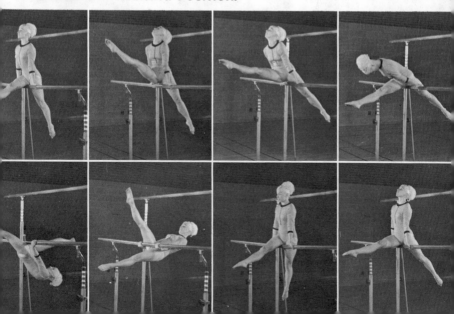

Cast, Single Leg Shoot Through (Single Leg Squat Through Arms)

With hands in a regular grip, cast upward from a front support position. At the top of the cast, bring one knee to the chest and tuck the leg. Keep arms straight and shoulders in front of the bar. Shoot the foot through the arms, keeping the back leg straight.

Press the shoulders back slightly to compensate for the leg going forward. Finish movement in a stride position with legs straight.

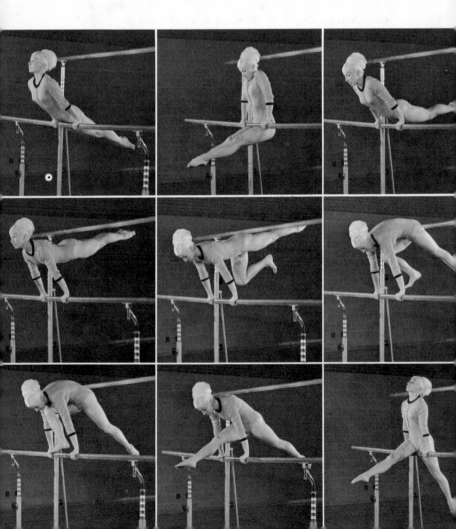

1. WITH HANDS IN REGULAR GRIP, CAST UPWARD FROM FRONT SUPPORT POSITION.
2. AT TOP OF CAST, BRING KNEE TO CHEST AND TUCK LEG.
3. KEEP ARMS STRAIGHT AND SHOULDERS IN FRONT OF BAR.
4. SHOOT FOOT THROUGH ARMS KEEPING BACK LEG STRAIGHT.
5. PRESS SHOULDERS BACK SLIGHTLY TO COMPENSATE FOR LEG GOING FORWARD.
6. FINISH IN STRIDE POSITION WITH LEGS STRAIGHT.

Back Hip Circle

With hands in a regular grip and from a front support position, cast. As body comes down and against the bar, relax the hips to let the legs come under the bar.

Lean back to follow the legs in a backward direction around the bar. Keep the arms straight and hips slightly piked.

Rotate around the bar to finish in a front support position.

1. WITH HANDS IN REGULAR GRIP AND FROM FRONT SUPPORT POSITION, CAST.
2. BRING BODY BACK DOWN AGAINST BAR.
3. RELAX HIPS, LETTING LEGS COME UNDER BAR.
4. LEAN BACK TO FOLLOW LEGS IN BACKWARD ROTATION AROUND BAR.
5. KEEP ARMS STRAIGHT AND HIPS SLIGHTLY PIKED.
6. ROTATE AROUND BAR TO FINISH IN FRONT SUPPORT POSITION.

Front Hip Circle

From a front support postion, with hands in a regular grip, stretch the body upward while supporting weight on the upper thighs, somewhat closer to the mid-thigh than for the regular front support.

Lean up and forward from the bar, keeping your arms straight. As the body falls forward, pike tightly putting your face toward your knees to rotate around the bar. Keep legs extended upward as body pikes.

Let hands slide around or momentarily release the bar to return to the top. Elbows are bent slightly as weight comes onto the arms and finish by bringing body and legs around the bar. Finish in a front support.

1. FROM FRONT SUPPORT WITH HANDS IN REGULAR GRIP, STRETCH BODY UPWARD WHILE SUPPORTING WEIGHT ON UPPER THIGHS.
2. LEAN UP AND FORWARD FROM THE BAR KEEPING ARMS STRAIGHT.
3. PIKE TIGHTLY AS BODY FALLS FORWARD.
4. KEEP LEGS EXTENDED UPWARD AS BODY PIKES.

5. **LET HANDS SLIDE AROUND THE BAR TO RETURN ON TOP.**
6. **ELBOWS ARE BENT SLIGHTLY AS WEIGHT COMES ONTO ARMS AND FINISH BRINGING LEGS AROUND BAR.**
7. **FINISH IN FRONT SUPPORT.**

Front Lying Cast to Squat on Low Bar

From a front lying position, with one hand in a regular grip on the low bar, swing legs under the low bar. Then cast upward pulling with the high bar hand.

Tuck knees to chest and place feet on the low bar. Finish in a squat on the low bar on balls of feet.

This movement also may be done by beginning with both hands on the high bar.

1. **FROM FRONT LYING POSITION WITH ONE HAND IN REGULAR GRIP ON LOW BAR, SWING LEGS UNDER LOW BAR.**
2. **CAST UPWARD BY PULLING WITH HAND ON UPPER BAR.**

3. TUCK KNEES TO CHEST AND PLACE BALLS
   OF FEET ON LOW BAR.
4. FINISH IN SQUAT ON LOW BAR.

Rear Support Half-Turn to Squat on Low Bar

From a rear support position on low bar, begin movement with one hand on the high bar, palm facing away from the body and opposite hand on the low bar in a regular grip.

Pull with the high bar hand while supporting weight on the low bar hand. Tuck knees to chest and pivot backward one-half turn around the low bar to place feet on the low bar in a squat position.

Finish the movement in a squat position on the low bar facing the high bar with one hand on the high bar in a regular grip and one hand on the low bar also in a regular grip.

1. FROM REAR SUPPORT, BEGIN WITH ONE HAND
   ON HIGH BAR, PALM FACING AWAY FROM
   BODY, AND WITH OPPOSITE HAND ON LOW
   BAR IN REGULAR GRIP.
2. PULL WITH HIGH BAR HAND WHILE
   SUPPORTING WEIGHT ON LOW BAR HAND.

3. TUCK KNEES TO CHEST AND PIVOT
   BACKWARD ONE-HALF TURN AROUND THE
   LOW BAR TO PLACE FEET ON LOW BAR IN
   SQUAT POSITION.
4. FINISH IN SQUAT POSITION ON LOW BAR
   FACING HIGH BAR WITH ONE HAND ON HIGH
   BAR IN REGULAR GRIP AND ONE HAND ON
   LOW BAR IN REGULAR GRIP.

Underswing Half-Turn Hip Circle from Sit

Sit on the low bar facing the high bar with hands in a crossed mixed grip (right palm facing body crossed behind left arm) and bar at back of the thighs.

Pull hard with your arms as you lift off the low bar. Extend toes to "reach" for high bar. As body extends upward and reaches the top of the swing, execute a half-turn to the left. Then swing in toward the low bar with body extended and legs slightly behind the hips.

As the hips hit the low bar and feet start to come around toward the face, release hands from the high bar to regrasp the low bar on each side of the hips. The body then circles backward, three-quarters around the low bar to finish in a front support.

1. SIT ON LOW BAR FACING HIGH BAR WITH
   HANDS IN CROSSED MIXED GRIP.
2. PULL HARD WITH ARMS AS YOU LIFT LEGS
   TOWARD HIGH BAR.
3. EXTEND TOES TO "REACH" FOR HIGH BAR.

4. AS BODY EXTENDS UPWARD AND REACHES TOP OF SWING, EXECUTE HALF-TURN TO LEFT.

5. SWING IN TOWARD LOW BAR WITH BODY EXTENDED AND LEGS SLIGHTLY BEHIND HIPS.

6 AS HIPS HIT LOW BAR AND FEET START TO COME AROUND TOWARD FACE, RELEASE HANDS FROM HIGH BAR TO REGRASP LOW BAR ON EACH SIDE OF HIPS.

7. CIRCLE AROUND LOW BAR TO FINISH IN FRONT SUPPORT.

Seat Swing
(Seat Rise or Peach)

From a rear support, lift body off the bar to a free "L" position with hands in regular grip.

Push the body back and downward to a free swing under the bar, keeping the body tightly piked with the shins near the face and the thighs away from the bar. The pike position is executed horizontally.

On the backswing, hold the pike and pull with straight arms to bring the body back to the top of the bar, open from the pike and finish in a rear support.

1. FROM REAR SUPPORT, LIFT BODY OFF BAR TO FREE "L" POSITION WITH HANDS IN REGULAR GRIP.
2. PUSH BODY BACK AND DOWNWARD TO FREE SWING UNDER BAR, KEEPING TIGHT PIKE WITH SHINS NEAR FACE AND THIGHS AWAY FROM BAR.
3. PIKE POSITION IS EXECUTED HORIZONTALLY.
4. ON BACKSWING, HOLD PIKE AND PULL WITH STRAIGHT ARMS TO BRING BODY BACK TO TOP OF BAR.
5. OPEN PIKE AND FINISH IN REAR SUPPORT.

Cast Off High Bar to Back Hip Circle on Low Bar

From front support on high bar facing low bar with hands in regular grip, cast up and out from the high bar. Maintain tight control of body and shoulders. With hips leading the legs swing down in a long hang to contact the low bar, with hips slightly ahead of the legs.

As legs swing toward face, release high bar to regrasp low bar. Circle backward around low bar to come to a front support position.

1. FROM FRONT SUPPORT ON HIGH BAR FACING LOW BAR WITH HANDS IN REGULAR GRIP, CAST UP AND OUT FROM HIGH BAR.

2. MAINTAIN TIGHT CONTROL OF BODY AND SHOULDERS.
3. WITH HIPS LEADING THE LEGS SLIGHTLY, SWING DOWN IN A LONG HANG TO CONTACT THE LOW BAR AT BEND OF HIPS.
4. BRING LEGS TOWARD FACE, AND RELEASE HIGH BAR REGRASPING ON LOW BAR.
5. CIRCLE BACKWARD AROUND BAR TO FINISH IN FRONT SUPPORT.

Flank Cut Regrasp on High Bar

From a rear support on high bar with hands in regular grip, lift the legs into a free pike position as body leans back. Swing under the bar keeping a tight pike horizontal to the floor.

Swing back up as for a seat swing movement. With shoulders above bar and arms straight, flank legs to right. Lift the right hand to allow the legs to pass over the bar then immediately regrasp the high bar with a regular grip. The left hand sustains the weight as the legs pass over the bar.

Finish in a long hang position on the high bar. This move may connect into a hip circle on low bar, a drop to a kip, or another position.

1. FROM REAR SUPPORT ON HIGH BAR WITH HANDS IN REGULAR GRIP, LIFT LEGS INTO FREE PIKE POSITION AS BODY LEANS BACK.
2. SWING UNDER BAR KEEPING TIGHT PIKE HORIZONTAL TO FLOOR.
3. SWING BACK UP AS FOR A SEAT SWING.

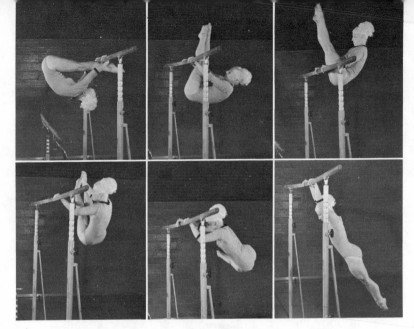

4. WITH SHOULDERS ABOVE BAR AND ARMS STRAIGHT, FLANK LEGS TO RIGHT.

5. LIFT RIGHT HAND TO ALLOW LEGS TO PASS OVER BAR THEN IMMEDIATELY REGRASP HIGH BAR WITH REGULAR GRIP. LEFT HAND SUSTAINS WEIGHT AS LEGS PASS OVER BAR.

6. FINISH IN LONG HANG POSITION ON HIGH BAR.

Kip Between the Bars (from Low Bar to High Bar)

From a rear support with hands in reverse grip, lift the legs into a pike with the body free of the bar. Keep the arms straight and allow the hands to slide forward and around the bar as the upper body is piked tightly to the legs.

Hold the pike as body circles the bar forward. Keep the bar at a position level with the back of the upper thigh. When returning to top of bar, hold the head and shoulders back as the legs are opened from pike.

Finish in rear support.

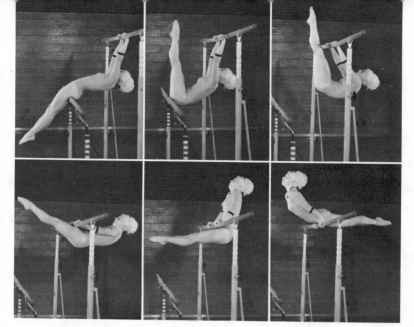

1. FROM REAR LYING SUPPORT WITH HANDS IN REGULAR GRIP ON HIGH BAR (SLIGHT OVERGRIP), EXTEND BODY SLIGHTLY DOWNWARD TO STRETCH SHOULDERS IN FRONT OF HIGH BAR.
2. PULL TOES TO HIGH BAR BY PIKING AT HIPS WITH ARMS STRAIGHT.
3. LEAN UPPER BODY FORWARD OVER HIGH BAR AS LEGS SWING DOWN AND BACK.
4. FINISH IN FRONT SUPPORT ON HIGH BAR.

Front Seat Circle

From a rear lying support on low bar with hands in a regular grip on high bar (slight overgrip), extend the body slightly downward to stretch the shoulders in front of the high bar.

Pull the toes to the high bar by piking at the hips with the arms straight. Lean the upper body forward and over the high bar as the legs swing down and back. End in a front support on the high bar.

A single or double leg stem rise is often a good lead up to this movement.

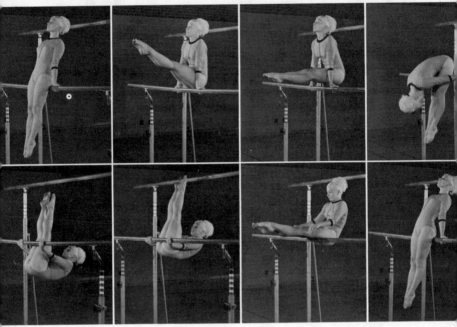

1. FROM REAR SUPPORT WITH HANDS IN REVERSE GRIP, LIFT LEGS INTO PIKE WITH BODY FREE OF BAR.
2. KEEP ARMS STRAIGHT AND ALLOW HANDS TO SLIDE FORWARD AROUND BAR AS UPPER BODY IS PIKED TIGHTLY TO LEGS.
3. HOLD PIKE AS BODY CIRCLES BAR FORWARD.
4. KEEP BAR AT POSITION LEVEL WITH BACK OF UPPER THIGH.
5. WHEN RETURNING TO TOP OF BAR, HOLD HEAD AND SHOULDERS BACK AS LEGS ARE LOWERED FROM PIKE.
6. FINISH IN REAR SUPPORT.

Back Seat Circle

From a rear support with hands in regular grip, lift the legs to a pike position free of the bar. Allow the hips to rotate slightly in front of bar as legs pike tightly toward face. Press backward and circle around bar, keeping bar at a level even with the back of the upper thigh.

At the bottom of circle, continue rotating hands around to the top of bar. The legs stay down and body uncurls. Head and shoulders are the last to open.

End in rear support with head and shoulders back.

1. **WITH HANDS IN REGULAR GRIP, LIFT LEGS TO PIKE FREE OF BAR FROM REAR SUPPORT POSITION.**
2. **ALLOW HIPS TO ROTATE SLIGHTLY IN FRONT OF BAR AS LEGS PIKE TIGHTLY TOWARD FACE.**
3. **PRESS BACKWARD AND CIRCLE AROUND BAR, KEEPING BAR AT A LEVEL EVEN WITH BACK OF UPPER THIGH.**
4. **AT BOTTOM OF CIRCLE, HANDS CONTINUE ROTATION TO TOP POSITION.**
5. **LEGS STAY DOWN AND BODY UNCURLS.**
6. **HEAD AND SHOULDERS LAST TO OPEN.**
7. **FINISH IN REAR SUPPORT WITH HEAD AND SHOULDERS BACK.**

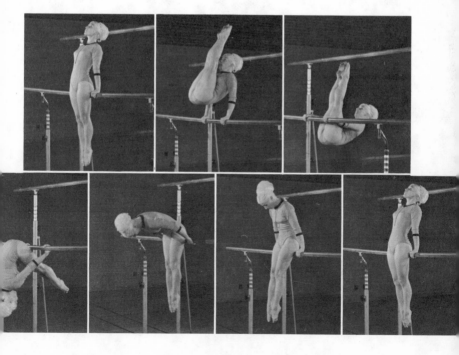

dismounts

The dismount is the last move which the judges see. It should be as impressive as possible, with good form and presentation. As in the mount, it is important to control and maintain the dismount without falling.

Single Leg Flank off Low Bar

With hands in a reverse grip and from a stride position (one leg extended between open hands in front of the low bar, other leg extended behind the low bar) lift body from bar. Swing the back leg over low bar, releasing the hand nearest back leg while the opposite arm supports your weight.

Bring legs together and execute a quarter turn. Finish in side stand position with one hand on low bar.

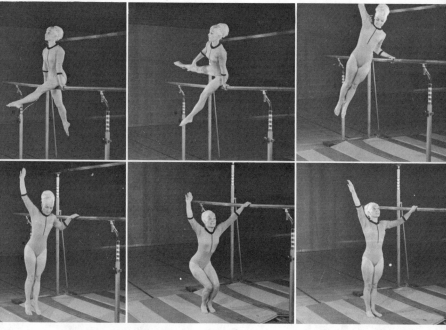

1. HANDS IN REVERSE GRIP.
2. IN A STRIDE POSITION, ONE LEG EXTENDS BETWEEN HANDS IN FRONT OF LOW BAR; THE OTHER LEG EXTENDS BEHIND BAR.
3. LIFT BODY FROM BAR.
4. SWING BACK LEG OVER LOW BAR, RELEASING HAND FROM THE BAR WHILE SUPPORTING WEIGHT WITH OPPOSITE HAND.
5. BRING LEGS TOGETHER AND EXECUTE A QUARTER TURN.
6. FINISH IN A SIDESTAND POSITION WITH ONE HAND ON LOW BAR.

Pike Forward Roll off High Bar

From a front support on high bar and hands in regular grip, rotate the hands around the bar as the body leans forward. While controlling a piked position and holding the weight on the arms, rotate the body off the high bar to a long hang.

Release the high bar and finish standing with your back to the low bar, slightly out from the high bar.

This dismount also may be executed from a tuck position.

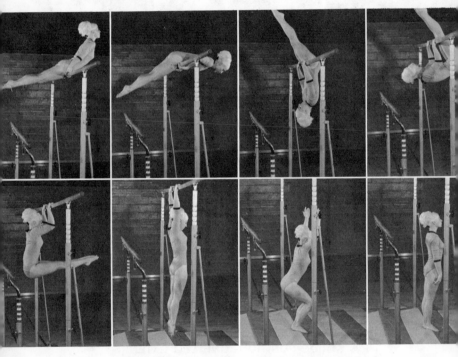

1. **FROM FRONT SUPPORT WITH HANDS IN REGULAR GRIP, ROTATE HANDS AROUND BAR AS BODY LEANS FORWARD.**
2. **CONTROL PIKED POSITION AND SUPPORT WEIGHT ON ARMS.**
3. **ROTATE BODY OFF HIGH BAR TO A LONG HANG.**
4. **RELEASE HIGH BAR AND FINISH DISMOUNT STANDING WITH BACK TO LOW BAR, SLIGHTLY AWAY FROM HIGH BAR.**

Back Straddle Sole Circle from Low Bar

Assume a straddle stand with arches of feet on low bar facing the high bar. One hand is in a regular grip on low bar, the other hand in a regular grip on the high bar. Pike at the hips then release the high bar hand to regrasp the low bar in a regular grip. Both hands are positioned between the straddled legs.

Keep legs straight and push feet against the low bar, while pulling with straight arms to create an equal stress. Press the buttocks back and downward, maintaining equal "push-pull" of legs and arms.

Circle backward three-fourths of the way around the low bar leading with the buttocks. Then relax the feet to push them upward and outward joining the legs at the top of arc while controlling the hips.

Release the hands from the low bar to allow your body to arch up, out and then down to land. End standing with your back to the low bar.

1. **ASSUME STRADDLE STAND WITH ARCHES OF FEET ON LOW BAR.**
2. **ONE HAND IN REGULAR GRIP ON LOW BAR; THE OTHER, IN REGULAR GRIP ON HIGH BAR.**
3. **PIKE AT HIPS.**
4. **RELEASE HIGH BAR HAND TO REGRASP LOW BAR WITH REGULAR GRIP. BOTH HANDS ARE BETWEEN STRADDLED LEGS.**

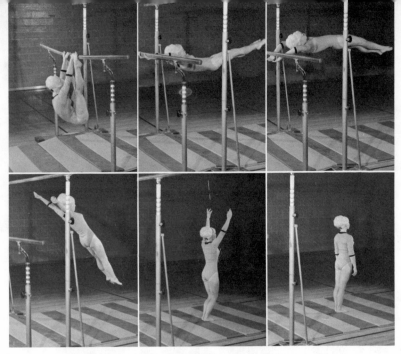

5. KEEP LEGS AND ARMS STRAIGHT, PUSH FEET AGAINST LOW BAR AND PULL WITH ARMS, CREATING AN EQUAL STRESS.

6. PUSH BUTTOCKS BACK AND DOWNWARD, MAINTAINING EQUAL "PUSH-PULL" OF THE ARMS AND LEGS.

7. LEADING WITH THE BUTTOCKS, CIRCLE BACKWARD THREE-FOURTHS OF WAY AROUND LOW BAR. RELAX FEET TO PUSH THEM UPWARD AND OUTWARD JOINING LEGS AT TOP OF ARC.

8. RELEASE HANDS FROM LOW BAR TO ALLOW BODY TO ARCH UP, OUT AND THEN DOWN TO LAND.

9. FINISH STANDING WITH BACK TO LOW BAR.

Squat over Low Bar

From a front support on low bar with hands in regular grip, swing the legs under the low bar then cast upward.

At the height of cast bend legs toward chest and squat the legs over the low bar, pushing hands and arms forward and upward off the low bar. Keep head and chest up. Finish in a stand with back to low bar.

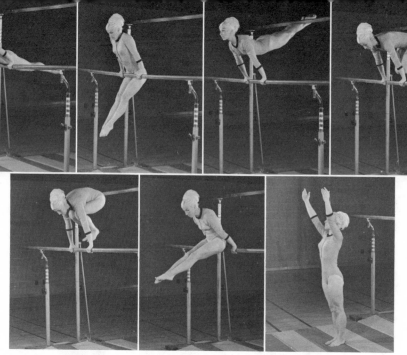

1. ASSUME FRONT SUPPORT POSITION WITH HANDS IN REGULAR GRIP.
2. SWING LEGS UNDER LOW BAR THEN CAST UPWARD.
3. BEND LEGS TOWARD CHEST AT TOP OF CAST AND SQUAT LEGS OVER LOW BAR.
4. PUSH HANDS AND ARMS FORWARD AND UPWARD OFF LOW BAR.
5. FINISH IN STAND WITH BACK TO LOW BAR.

Flank Cut off High Bar

From a rear support with hands in regular grip, lift the body into a pike, free of the bar. Swing down under bar executing a seat swing and then back up.

With shoulders above the bar, press down on straight arms and flank legs to right so as to release the right hand.

As legs swing down to a vertical position, release the left hand to land on the mat. Finish in a stand behind the high bar with left side to the bars.

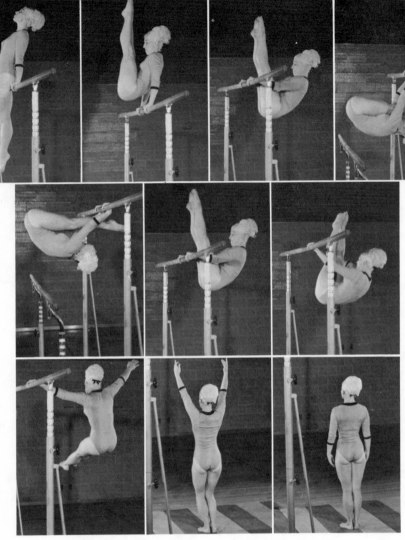

1. FROM REAR SUPPORT WITH HANDS IN REGULAR GRIP, LIFT BODY INTO PIKE FREE OF BAR.
2. SWING UNDER BAR AND THEN BACK UP.
3. WHEN SHOULDERS ARE ABOVE THE BAR, PRESS DOWN ON STRAIGHT ARMS AND FLANK LEGS TO RIGHT THEN RELEASE RIGHT HAND.
4. AS LEGS SWING DOWN TO VERTICAL POSITION, RELEASE LEFT HAND TO LAND ON MAT.
5. FINISH IN A STAND BEHIND HIGH BAR WITH LEFT SIDE TO BAR.

Dimensions

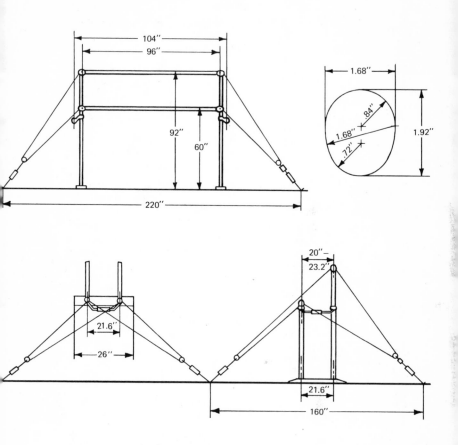

rules simplified

There is no time limit on the uneven parallel bars; however, each routine should contain a mount, 8 to 10 movements and a dismount. Compositionally, the routine should be predominantly swinging moves. It should show movements on both bars, facing both directions. It should have movements above and below the bars. There should be moments of nonsupport as well as supports on various parts of the body.

Positive or Negative Methods of Scoring

Judging may be done in one of two mathematical methods. One method awards points while the other subtracts deductions.

The practice of adding up the deductions and subtracting them from the point allotment for each category is referred to as *negative scoring*.

EXAMPLE:	POINTS ALLOWED	DEDUCTIONS
Difficulty	4.0	—0.5
Origin. & Value of Comb.	1.5	—0.8
Composition	0.5	—0.2
Execution	1.5	—0.8
Amplitude	1.5	—1.0
General Impression	1.0	—0.4
TOTAL	10.0	—3.7

The total 3.7 in deductions is subtracted from the possible 10.0 points to arrive at the final score for the gymnast of 6.3 points.

The method of awarding points to the gymnast in each of the categories according to how well she executed or met the requirements of that category is employing the technique of *positive scoring*.

EXAMPLE:	POINTS ALLOWED	POINTS AWARDED
Difficulty	4.0	3.5
Origin. & Value of Comb.	1.5	0.7
Composition	0.5	0.3
Execution	1.5	0.7
Amplitude	1.5	0.5
General Impression	1.0	0.6
TOTAL	10.0	6.3

The total of 6.3 points is the final score and would be used as the gymnast's score.

The negative method of scoring is best used to score an advanced, highly skilled gymnast. Obviously the better caliber gymnast will make fewer mistakes, and your mathematics will be much easier working with the small numbers of the few deductions.

Scoring information courtesy of National Federation of State High School Associations.

For Complete and Up-To-Date Rules and Scoring Information, Consult These Sources:

Amateur Athletic Union (AAU)
3400 W. 86th Street
Indianapolis, Indiana 46268

F.I.G. Code of Points for Women
U.S. Gymnastics Federation
P.O. Box 4699
Tucson, Arizona 85717

Division for Girls'
and Women's Sports
1201 Sixteenth St., N.W.
Washington, D.C. 20036

National Federation of State
High School Associations
P.O. Box 98
Elgin, Illinois 60120

glossary of gymnastics terms

AAU—Amateur Athletic Union of the United States.

Aerial—A stunt or dance move done in the air free of support.

All-Around—Women's four Olympic events: balance beam, floor exercise, uneven parallel bars and vaulting.

All-Around Champion—Highest scoring gymnast using the all-around events. Considered to be the best gymnast in that particular meet or competition.

Attitude—A leg position; a leg in front or behind the body. The knee is bent with the leg turned out parallel to the floor.

Compulsory Routine—A prescribed routine. Written in detail, it must be performed as written with certain exceptions.

DGWS—Division for Girls' and Women's Sports. A part of the American Association for Health, Physical Education and Recreation (AHPER).

FIG—International Gymnastic Federation. A governing body for international gymnastics.

Flip—A term used synonymously with somersault or salto meaning to turn over in the air.

Head Judge—Judge designated to be the head of the other judges on a particular event.

Inverted Support—A position of support upside-down. Support may be on the hands or head.

IOC—International Olympic Committee. The governing body of the Olympic Games.

Kip—A movement or action where the body pikes and extends rapidly.

Lay Out—A body position. The body is extended in an almost straight line, the back is only very slightly arched.

Nationals—Term used to describe United States National Gymnastic Championships held once a year.

Oblique—A position of the arms in relation to the body. Usually halfway between the horizontal and vertical. It may be in front, behind or at the side of the body.

Optional Routine—A creative exercise or routine composed by the coach, the gymnast or both.

Pan Am's—Pan American Games. Competition between the American continents includes gymnastic events.

Pike—A body position in which the hips are bent so that the thighs are near the chest. Usually done with straight legs.

Punch—An explosive action off the feet or hands. Very quickly getting off the floor or apparatus. A short, powerful action.

Reuther board—A takeoff board which gets its spring by a slight flex in the wood. It is slightly inclined to aid in changing forward momentum to upward momentum.

Salto—A term for aerial somersault or flip. Used in European texts and getting more use in the United States. May be done forward, backward or sideward.

Scratch—To remove a name from the list of competitors in a meet.

Side Horse—Piece of equipment. Used by women for vaulting, it is used width-wise.

Specialist—A gymnast who concentrates on one or two events instead of going "all-around." A specialist usually may not compete in National Championships unless she competes all-around.

Stick—To land from a dismount or vault without loss of balance or movement of the feet.

Stoop—To pass the legs through the arms without bending the knees.

Straddle—A leg position. The legs are spread wide apart.

Superior Judge—In higher level competition, the fifth judge. She is usually more qualified than the other four judges and her score counts if there is a dispute.

Tour—To turn. May be done in air or on floor or on apparatus.

Tuck—A body position. Bend the knees to the chest, round the back and keep heels close to the buttocks.

USGF—United States Gymnastic Federation. A governing body for gymnastics in the United States.

USOC—United States Olympic Committee. The governing body for the Olympic Games in the United States.

World Games—Competition between the nations of the world. Held between the Olympic years.

notes